GW00633006

CANALS

The Francis Frith Collection

First published in the United Kingdom in 2006 by
The Francis Frith Collection

ISBN 1-84589-082-5

British Library Cataloguing in Publication Data

Francis Frith's 50 Classics - Canals
Compiled by Terence and Eliza Sackett

The Francis Frith Collection
Frith's Barn, Teffont,
Salisbury, Wiltshire SP3 5QP
Tel: +44 (0) 1722 716 376
Email: info@francisfrith.co.uk
www.francisfrith.co.uk

Printed and bound in India

Front Cover: **LLANGOLLEN**, *On the Canal 1913* 65830t
The colour-tinting is for illustrative purposes only, and is not intended to be historically accurate

FRANCIS FRITH
VICTORIAN PIONEER

Francis Frith, founder of the world-famous photographic archive, was a complex and multi-talented man. A devout Quaker and a highly successful Victorian businessman, he was philosophic by nature and pioneering in outlook. By 1855 he had already established a wholesale grocery business in Liverpool, and sold it for the astonishing sum of £200,000, which is the equivalent today of over £15,000,000. Now in his thirties, and captivated by the new science of photography, Frith set out on a series of pioneering journeys up the Nile and to the Near East.

INTRIGUE AND EXPLORATION

He was the first photographer to venture beyond the sixth cataract of the Nile. Africa was still the mysterious 'Dark Continent', and Stanley and Livingstone's historic meeting was a decade into the future. The conditions for picture taking confound belief. He laboured for hours in his wicker dark-room in the sweltering heat of the desert, while the volatile chemicals fizzed dangerously in their trays. Back in London he exhibited his photographs and was 'rapturously cheered' by members of the Royal Society. His reputation as a photographer was made overnight.

VENTURE OF A LIFE-TIME

By the 1870s the railways had threaded their way across the country, and Bank Holidays and half-day Saturdays had been made obligatory by Act of Parliament. All of a sudden the working man and his family were able to enjoy days out, take holidays, and see a little more of the world.

With typical business acumen, Francis Frith foresaw that these new tourists would enjoy having souvenirs to commemorate their days out. For the next thirty years he travelled the country by train and by pony and trap, producing fine photographs of seaside resorts and beauty spots that were keenly bought by millions of Victorians.

These prints were painstakingly pasted into family albums and pored over during the dark nights of winter, rekindling precious memories of summer excursions. Frith's studio was soon supplying retail shops all over the country, and by 1890 F Frith & Co had become the greatest specialist photographic publishing company in the world, with over 2,000 sales outlets, and pioneered the picture postcard.

FRANCIS FRITH'S LEGACY

Francis Frith had died in 1898 at his villa in Cannes, his great project still growing. The archive he created continued in business for another seventy years. By 1970 it contained over a third of a million pictures showing 7,000 British towns and villages.

Frith's legacy to us today is of immense significance and value, for the magnificent archive of evocative photographs he created provides a unique record of change in the cities, towns and villages throughout Britain over a century and more.

Frith and his fellow studio photographers revisited locations many times down the years to update their views, compiling for us an enthralling and colourful pageant of British life and character.

We are fortunate that Frith was dedicated to recording the minutiae of everyday life. For it is this sheer wealth of visual data, the painstaking chronicle of changes in dress, transport, street layouts, buildings, housing, engineering and landscape that captivates us so much today, offering us a powerful link with the past and with the lives of our ancestors.

Computers have now made it possible for Frith's many thousands of images to be accessed almost instantly. The archive offers every one of us an opportunity to examine the places where we and our families have lived and worked down the years. Its images, depicting our shared past, are now bringing pleasure and enlightenment to millions around the world a century and more after his death.

INTRODUCTION

This colourful pocket book contains 50 classic Frith photographs of canals and life on the water from all over the country. It depicts the essence of the rich and varied life of our canal network in an era when they were major arteries for the transportation of freight.

You'll find fascinating period scenes of peaceful country canals, and bustling views of canals in towns and cities; there are horse-drawn and motorised narrow boats, bridges, locks, towpaths, aqueducts and a boat lift—in fact, all the picturesque paraphernalia of canal life as it was in an era long since passed. Each of the photographs is accompanied by an informative caption.

Evocative and atmospheric, these stunning images will transport you back into a bygone age on the water, revealing our canals not only as picturesque waterways but as extraordinary and pioneering feats of engineering.

This tiny stretch, less than a mile long, is all that is left of the grandiose Portsmouth & Arundel Canal, which linked Ford on the River Arun with Chichester and Portsmouth Harbour. It opened in 1823, but soon faced local opposition when the residents complained that seawater was seeping from it into their wells and contaminating the drinking water. The company ignored the protests, but failed to drum up trade, and the canal was derelict by the 1860s.

A little-known fact is that Exeter was the first place to be served by an artificial canal with locks. This, constructed in 1564-66, pre-dated the canals in the north of England, where many people think the canal age started. It was built after the building of a weir in the 13th century at Countess Wear stopped the use of the river for trade.

DEVON, THE EXETER SHIP CANAL 1929 82302 2

Exeter's canal was built at the request of the city's Tudor merchants and traders, who were exasperated by the weirs on the River Exe that obstructed the free flow of water transport into the city. John Trew's pioneering canal was minuscule, just 3 feet deep and 16 feet wide. It boasted the first pound locks in Britain. In the 1820s, James Green widened the canal considerably, carving it out to a depth of 15 feet so that it could carry vessels of several hundred tons up to the city canal basin. Yet it never truly prospered after these costly improvements, for the city's woollen export trade declined. This approach to the city is picturesque, with the canal winding its way through the meadows between reed-fringed banks.

The Grand Western Canal was a 19th-century dream, planned to run from Taunton to the River Exe near Exeter. In the event, the main line from Taunton was built as a tub boat canal with a very short life, and an 11-mile stretch from Loudwells to Tiverton was built as a barge canal. Tiverton was actually a branch from the main line. Today, you can take a trip on this section aboard a horse-drawn barge from Tiverton.

DEVON, TIVERTON, ON THE CANAL 1903 49613

4

Bude's canal, built in 1823, was something of an oddity. For its first two miles, it was a barge canal – as seen here. Then, freight was trans-shipped into small 5-ton tubs with wheels. These were horse-drawn; but instead of using locks, the tub boats were hauled up and down inclined planes by engine to reach the different water levels. By the 1830s over thirty miles of canal had been constructed, which was used to transport 50,000 tons of sea sand a year from the north Cornwall coast for use as fertiliser on inland farms.

5

CORNWALL, THE BUDE CANAL 1920 69567

This was the only English canal to open directly into the Atlantic Ocean. Bude sea lock is still in use today, although the rest of the canal was abandoned in 1896. However, the barge section was retained as a water channel.

Devizes is perched on the top of a hill overlooking the Avon valley. From there, the Kennet & Avon Canal plunges down the extraordinary flight of 29 locks at Caen Hill to the valley below. The pattern created by the extending balance beams has been compared to the backbone of a huge reptile. This lock is on the edge of town, close to the old prison.

This set of 16 locks is part of the famous flight of 29 at Caen Hill. These locks are so close together that in order to maintain a satisfactory supply of water, it was necessary to extend the canal at the left-hand side above each chamber. These are known as side ponds. Each time the flight is operated, 11 million gallons of water disappear downhill!

9   GLOUCESTERSHIRE, CHALFORD, THE THAMES & SEVERN CANAL 1910 62711

Now derelict, the Thames & Severn Canal linked the two rivers. It was specially built to accommodate the elegant sailing barges called Severn trows. The canal closed in 1954. As it climbs the area known as Golden Valley, the scenery is magnificent.

The Monmouthshire Canal ran from Newport to Pontymoile, with a branch to Crumlin. Allt-yr-yn is the name of the hill in the distance. The lock chambers on this canal had their own individual size, 64ft 9in x 9ft 2ins – a most peculiar gauge. The canal became disused in 1930. At the top of the flight is a Visitor Centre with plenty of information, and it is possible to walk down the flight.

Lydney's minuscule canal is no more than a mile in length, with just a single lock. Pictured here are barges carrying timber from Avonmouth Docks to the industrial yard on the left. The trade declined in the 1970s.

This canal was constructed in 1796; it runs for nearly forty miles through northern Hampshire. It was never a financial success because of its rural course, and the success of the Kennet & Avon Canal put paid to the owners' hopes. Here we see the upper reaches, and the surface weed indicates a lack of commercial use. Note the telegraph poles on the left, once a regular sight alongside canals. Today they have gone; beneath the towpath, fibre optic cables are now buried – today's version of another kind of communication.

In 1651, Sir Richard Weston of nearby Sutton Place embarked on his great enterprise to create the Wey Navigation and make the river commercially navigable from Guildford to the Thames, by straightening out some of the many meanders in its course and installing pound locks. With the labour of two hundred men and the expenditure of £15,000, in nine months ten of the fourteen miles to Weybridge were complete. Over the next century this route formed the principal outlet for the timber, grain, wool and other products of the area centred on Guildford. The stacks of timber on the opposite bank (centre) show, in this view downstream to the lock, that even at the start of the 20th century the Wey Navigation had an important role to play in the local economy.

This view shows
an early example
of a houseboat.
As an inexpensive
home, converted
narrowboats are
still popular,
especially closer
to Oxford, where
there are dozens to
be seen.

The Oxford Canal was first opened as far as Banbury in 1778 and to Oxford in 1790. It is a classic example of contour cutting by the engineer Samuel Simcock: there are no locks, because the canal hugs the contours of the land. It is a pretty, meandering line, very popular with holidaymakers.

When the Oxford Canal finally reached Oxford in 1790, the city bells were rung to celebrate the arrival of the first barges loaded with coal from Coventry. This photograph perfectly depicts the incomparable power of the countryside canal to conjure up peace and contentment. The boat is a disused butty, the 'Doris', and she makes a fine perch for the anglers. The peace and quiet they are obviously enjoying has gone now: it is shattered by the M40 motorway close by.

Here we see two horse-drawn narrow boats, the 'Linnet' and the 'Evelyn', belonging to George Garside, at the attractively sited lock in Cassiobury Park, Watford. The horse on the left is waiting to haul the boats, which are 'breasted up' together in the lock. This was just one lock in the long climb from the west edge of London up the Chilterns: there were 25 miles and 42 locks on the Grand Junction Canal (later to become part of the Grand Union), the original main transport artery between London and Birmingham.

The Aylesbury arm of the Grand Union departs from the main line at Marsworth, and has some 16 locks in 6 miles, very narrow and not for the faint-hearted. Here, children are trying their luck at fishing in the Aylesbury Arm of the Grand Union Canal. Just beyond the bridge is the delightfully named Hills and Partridges Lock.

Here we see a pair of loaded working boats on the Aylesbury Arm near Broughton on the edge of town.
The wooden stumps (bottom left) are known as strapping posts, and were used to tie up boats. Their state in this
view appears to be somewhat poor. Two ladies, dressed in the fashions of the day, take their ease.

These are Soulbury Three Locks on the Grand Union Canal north of Leighton Buzzard. The lady is using the rope over the gate to take the last forward movement off the butty boat. Note that the top gate on the second chamber is already open, ready for them. The white building is the Three Locks pub, built to serve canal boatmen.

BEDFORDSHIRE, LEIGHTON BUZZARD, THE THREE LOCKS, THE GRAND UNION CANAL C1955 L211054

A craft heads southwards towards Blisworth Tunnel on the Grand Union Canal. The tunnel, 3,057 yards long, is the longest currently open to all boats; it is said that the silence inside is 'appalling' and 'deathly still'. The pretty tower of the 14th-century church is clearly visible here.

The Frith archive originally recorded this photograph as being taken at Oldbury, but this is patently not so. The boat on the right is wide beamed: that narrows the area for consideration somewhat. The best guess is that we are just below Copper Mill Lock at Harefield on the Grand Union Canal. The pair of horse-drawn boats (the left-hand one is the 'Blyth') were owned by Thomas Clayton of Oldbury, who specialised in carrying waste products from the gas industry. They are heading towards the bank, where the man in the bow will heave his line to the shore - the horse is being led along the towpath to be hitched up again.

A motorised narrow boat tows its butty along behind — on the open canal, the 'snubber' or towing rope was normally 60 feet long. They are heading south on the Grand Union Canal from Braunston Tunnel. At Braunston the canal drops sharply through six locks. The somewhat precarious towing path seen here has been reinstated now, and forms part of the long-distance London to Birmingham footpath.

James Brindley created this successful canal in 1772. It was a vital part of the Grand Cross network that linked the rivers Trent, Servern, Thames and Mersey. The church of St Mary and All Saints looks delightful; it is built from local red sandstone. The warehouse beneath is owned by the London Midland & Scottish Railway Company; one of the boats is mooored close by. To the right, a lorry is just visible, loading the coal from the Baggeridge Colliery yard.

Though it passes through an industrial landscape, this canal has many quiet rural stretches where the narrow boats chug along under a dense canopy of green. Unlike many of its rivals, the Staffordshire & Worcestershire never sold out to the railway companies, some of whom made a policy of buying up canals, then running them down so that they could gradually take over the freight business. At Kinver, a lofty wooded red sandstone ridge offers delightful views over the Staffordshire countryside.

STAFFORDSHIRE, KINVER, THE STAFFORDSHIRE & WORCESTERSHIRE CANAL C1955 K37080

25

At Great Haywood Junction, the Trent & Mersey meet the Staffordshire & Worcestershire Canal. Clay was shipped along this canal to Wedgewood's potteries, and on the return trip the barges were slow but sure transport for the fragile china. At the northern end of the Staffordshire & Worcestershire Canal, an unusual pleasure boat conversion heads towards Wolverhampton. The narrow section is a solid aqueduct over the River Trent. Shugborough Hall, Lord Lichfield's house, is behind the trees to the left; the small building on the towing path is now a craft shop.

STAFFORDSHIRE, GREAT HAYWOOD,
THE STAFFORDSHIRE & WORCESTERSHIRE CANAL C1955 G303010

Created in 1790, this successful canal was built to ship Bedworth coal to the town of Coventry. At Hopwas, just beyond Tamworth, the canal threads its way through attractive wooded country.

On the Chelmer & Blackwater Navigation, barges carried timber and coals. The rivers Chelmer and Blackwater meet in Maldon; this cut was built in 1797 to enable ships to reach Chelmsford. This waterway was one of the last to be dug, and had a short commercial life because of successful poaching of its business by the railways. At Heybridge Basin, near Maldon, huge colliery barges offloaded their coal for onward delivery to Chelmsford. Many returned loaded with timber or manure. Here we see a plodding horse hauling a shallow-draught barge with its load of lime, with Beeleigh Flood Lock in the background.

Wisbech's five mile-long canal once connected the villages of Outwell and Upwell with the River Nene at Wisbech. It has since been filled in and closed down. Wisbech is the capital of the Fens. It was once a strategic seaport, where coasters transhipped their cargoes into fenland lighters. Yet the tides have played the town foul over the centuries, silting up successive estuaries of the River Nene so that now the town is stranded ten miles from the sea. However, ships still struggle in to berth at the quaysides of the town. At low tide they are knee deep in mud. In this view of the canal, the old lock is in the background.

CAMBRIDGESHIRE, WISBECH, THE WISBECH CANAL 1929 81972

29

The Anderton Boat Lift linked the Trent & Mersey Canal with the River Weaver. Narrow boats entered a caisson along the trough to the left and were lowered down to the river. One such can be seen sandwiched between two barges. The Anderton Lift created a much faster passage for boats and increased the tonnage of river traffic to 226,000 in 1913. It was converted to electric power in 1906 and extensively renovated in 1974.

The Shropshire Union Canal was owned by a railway, the LMS, and was formed in 1864. It runs between Wolverhampton and Ellesmere Port. A narrow canal, it passes through delightful countryside, and maintains a level for twenty miles until it reaches Wheaton Aston. The lock keeper's cottage (left of photograph) is now a private house, and the large building behind has gone.

STAFFORDSHIRE, WHEATON ASTON,
THE SHROPSHIRE UNION CANAL C1955 W286009

31

SHROPSHIRE, MARKET DRAYTON,
THE SHROPSHIRE UNION CANAL, TYRLEY LOCKS 1911 63346

Below the second Tyrley lock, a loaded narrow boat poses for the camera. The man would work the locks, the little girl would drive the horse, and the mother would steer: this was a family business. As for the children attending school, forget it! Life was hard for the one-man operation. Bargemen worked a six- or seven-day week, received no sick pay and had no salary during freeze-ups. Yet they doubtless relished their independence — and the beautiful scenery.

The Shropshire Union ran successfully from 1864 to the Second World War. Heading south, having just emerged from the Tyrley Locks near Market Drayton, is a narrow boat that has been converted to a tanker belonging to Thomas Clayton of Oldbury. These boats carried Shell oil from Ellesmere Port from 1924 until shortly after this picture was taken.

The boat we saw in photograph M32031R (No 33) is now seen climbing the 5 locks at Tyrley. From here, there was a lock-free run all the way to the edge of Wolverhampton - apart from the one at Wheaton Aston which we saw earlier (No 31). After that, there was a flight of 21 before a short dash to the company's base, where the cargo would be pumped out. The boats used to take a week to do the round trip of some 160 miles.

**SHROPSHIRE, MARKET DRAYTON,
THE SHROPSHIRE UNION CANAL, TYRLEY LOCKS** c1955 M32035

CLWYD, LLANGOLLEN, THE LLANGOLLEN CANAL 1913 65830

This woodland on the Llangollen Canal just outside the town exists today, and the canal's channel has been extensively improved. What is now Britain's most popular cruising canal was actually built as a water supply to the Ellesmere Canal further downstream.

Constructed by Telford and Jessop to link the rivers Severn, Dee and Mersey, the Llangollen Canal is one of the most popular waterways in the country. Here we see the River Ceiriog, which is also the border between England and Wales: the cameraman is on the Welsh side. The aqueduct, a most impressive stone structure built in 1801, soars 70 feet above the river. Its majesty was attenuated somewhat when the Great Western Railway line from Wolverhampton to Chester came along and was built even higher.

The Duke of Bridgewater has been called 'the parent and father' of our canal system. In 1760 he employed the pioneering engineer James Brindley to create a waterway connecting his coal mines with Manchester. This is a historic view, as these locks, linking the Manchester Ship Canal and the Bridgewater Canal, were infilled in 1966. There were ten chambers, each one duplicated to speed the flow of traffic.

A pair of boats prepares to enter a lock. The left-hand one – the 'Stafford' – sports its Fellows, Morton & Clayton livery, a company that stopped trading when the canals were nationalised in 1948. The right-hand boat is the 'Shad', an ex-FMC motor in the colour of its new owners.

The Bridgewater Canal flows through the pretty town of Lymm in Cheshire. An empty pair of boats (the one in front is the 'Clio') head towards Manchester, probably to collect coal. It is unusual that the butty has no steerer, although the tiller is in place. Perhaps he/she had just popped below to put the kettle on. Heating and cooking was performed on a coal-fired range, whose chimney we can see behind the tiller. On the right, in front of the bridge, there is a lifting winch.

A pair of Horsfield's craft are carrying coal, the once horse-drawn butty (the 'Marjorie') towed by the motorised narrow boat. By the time this photograph was taken, commercial carrying in narrow boats was almost at an end; it was kept going in many cases by early canal enthusiasts, for whom working long anti-social hours in all weathers was actually a pleasure.

CHESHIRE, LYMM, THE BRIDGEWATER CANAL c1960 L122054

The city of Manchester was the powerhouse of northern industry. The fact that all of its manufacturing products had to be shipped through the port of Liverpool – Manchester's arch-rival – dented the city fathers' pride. They demanded an outlet to the sea, and got one in 1894 at a cost of over £14,000,000. This superb new seaway, with its deep-water berths, brought Manchester a huge trading advantage.

One impressive feature of the Manchester Ship Canal was the Barton Aqueduct, designed by Edward Leader Williams. It carried the Bridgewater Canal across the new waterway, and pivoted on a central support.

GREATER MANCHESTER, BARTON UPON IRWELL,
BARTON AQUEDUCT 1894 33693

Here we see the phenomenally busy Sheffield Basin, at the end of the Sheffield & South Yorkshire Navigation. Two of the boats have large masts, making them Yorkshire sailing keels, a type of boat popular in the North East years ago; they were sturdily built with oak planks up to 3 inches thick, and transported coals and industrial products. Everything here has changed. The Basin is now Victoria Quays, and leisure development is all. The Great Central Railway sidings to the right have also disappeared.

With its 29 automated locks, this modern, commercial waterway forms a link with sea-going ships at the port of Goole. The Sheffield & South Yorkshire was established in 1895, and was created from a grouping of several much older waterways, including the Stainforth & Keady and the Sheffield canals.

At 127 miles, this is the longest canal in Britain, and creates a vital trans-Pennine crossing between the mill towns of Yorkshire and the seaports of the Mersey. The famous Five Rise locks raise barges and boats an awesome 60 feet. This splendid view shows both the flight and boats. The furthest boat is a steam-powered tug, which will move the immaculate coal-laden transom-sterned 'short boat' with sweeping lines and long wooden tiller. It could carry a load twice the size of a narrow boat. Note the fancy rope-work on the stern: it is clean, despite the dirty cargo.

BINGLEY, THE LEEDS & LIVERPOOL CANAL C1900 B98501

Work on the Leeds & Liverpool began in 1770. Not only did the coming of the canal vastly lower distribution costs for the industrial towns of Yorkshire, it also provided a localised transport service for the towns and cities through which it passed. Skipton was linked up in 1773 as part of the relatively simple first section, which needed no locks. The sections from Leeds to Gargrave and from Wigan to Liverpool followed by 1777. Then the funding ran out. For years progress was slow, but the missing stages were finally completed in 1816.

YORKSHIRE, SKIPTON WOODS,
THE LEEDS & LIVERPOOL CANAL C1955 S137026

Ripon is the farthest north a barge can travel without being removed from the water. This short, 2-mile canal was opened in 1773, and is an extension of the River Ure. In this view of the stone-walled canal basin we see the cathedral rising over the roofs, and the old arched bridge.

The Lancaster Canal was never connected to the main canal system. Its rugged stone bridges and its proximity to the Pennines make it a most picturesque line. Carnforth is towards the northern end; the top section was abandoned after the M6 motorway was built. Here we see a barge loaded down with hay, with the two horses taking a break as the photographer creates his picture.

LANCASHIRE, CARNFORTH, THE LANCASTER CANAL 1918 68306

Lancaster's beautiful canal, with its magnificent sea views of Morecambe Bay, was originally the vision of the factory owners of the locality, who were eager to connect their mills with the national canal network via the Bridgewater. Stone, slate and lime would be carried from the north, and Wigan coal from the south. By 1819 the designer John Rennie had constructed a canal from Kendal in the north down to Wigan, a canal remarkable for the ingenuity of its design.

INDEX

FREE PRINT OF YOUR CHOICE

Choose any Frith photograph in this book.

Simply complete the Voucher opposite and return it with your remittance for £2.25 (to cover postage and handling) and we will print the photograph of your choice in SEPIA (size 11 x 8 inches) and supply it in a cream mount with a burgundy rule line (overall size 14 x 11 inches).

Please note: photographs with a reference number starting with a "Z" are not Frith photographs and cannot be supplied under this offer.

Offer valid for delivery to one UK address only.

PLUS: **Order additional Mounted Prints at HALF PRICE - £7.49 each** (normally £14.99)

If you would like to order more Frith prints from this book, possibly as gifts for friends and family, you can buy them at half price (with no additional postage and handling costs).

PLUS: **Have your Mounted Prints framed**

For an extra £14.95 per print you can have your mounted print(s) framed in an elegant polished wood and gilt moulding, overall size 16 x 13 inches (no additional postage and handling required).

FRITH PRODUCTS AND SERVICES

All Frith photographs are available for you to buy as framed or mounted prints. From time to time, other illustrated items such as Address Books and Maps are also available. Already, almost 100,000 Frith archive photographs can be viewed and purchased on the internet through the Frith website.

For more detailed information on Frith companies and products, visit:

www.francisfrith.co.uk

Mounted Print
Overall size 14 x 11 inches (355 x 280mm)

IMPORTANT!

These special prices are only available if you use this form to order. You must use the ORIGINAL VOUCHER (no copies permitted).

We can only despatch to one UK address. This offer cannot be combined with any other offer.

For further information, contact:

The Francis Frith Collection, Frith's Barn,

Teffont, Salisbury SP3 5QP

Tel: +44 (0) 1722 716 376

Fax: +44 (0) 1722 716 881

Email: sales@francisfrith.co.uk

Send completed *Voucher form to:*

The Francis Frith Collection, Frith's Barn, Teffont, Salisbury, Wiltshire SP3 5QP England

If you need more space, please write your address on a separate sheet of paper.

Voucher

for FREE and Reduced Price Frith Prints

Do not photocopy this voucher. Only the original is valid, so please fill it in, cut it out and return it to us with your order.

Picture ref no	Page number	Qty	Mounted @ £7.49	Framed + £14.95	Order Total £
1		1	Free of charge*	£	£
2			£7.49	£	£
3			£7.49	£	£
4			£7.49	£	£
5			£7.49	£	£
6			£7.49	£	£
			*Post & handling	£2.25	
			Total Order Cost		£

Title of this book . . . .

Please allow 28 days for delivery.
Offer available to one UK address only

I enclose a cheque / postal order for £ . . . .
payable to 'The Francis Frith Collection'

OR debit my Mastercard / Visa / Maestro card

Card Number

Issue No (Maestro only)   Valid from (Maestro)

Expires   Signature

Name Mr/Mrs/Ms . . . .

Address . . . .

. . . . Postcode. . . . .

Daytime Tel No . . . .

E-mail . . . .

ISBN 1-84589-082-5   Valid to 31/12/08